W9-CFB-488

C. H. Booth Library
25 Main Street
Newtown, CT 06470

EDGE BOOKS™

SPORTS RIVALRIES

OUTRAGEOUS

CAR RACING
RIVALRIES

BY TRACY NELSON MAURER

CONSULTANT: SUZANNE WISE, LIBRARIAN, BELK LIBRARY, STOCK CAR RACING COLLECTION,
APPALACHIAN STATE UNIVERSITY, BOONE, NORTH CAROLINA

CAPSTONE PRESS
a capstone imprint

Edge Books are published by Capstone Press,
1710 Roe Crest Drive, North Mankato, Minnesota 56003
www.capstonepub.com

Copyright © 2015 by Capstone Press, a Capstone imprint. All rights reserved.
No part of this publication may be reproduced in whole or in part, or stored in a
retrieval system, or transmitted in any form or by any means, electronic, mechanical,
photocopying, recording, or otherwise, without written permission of the publisher.

Library of Congress Cataloging-in-Publication Data
Cataloging-in-publication information is on file with the Library of Congress.
ISBN 978-1-4914-2025-6 (library binding)
ISBN 978-1-4914-2196-3 (eBook PDF)

Editorial Credits
Angie Kaelberer and Alesha Sullivan, editors; Ted Williams, designer;
Eric Gohl, media researcher; Tori Abraham, production specialist

Photo Credits
AP Photo: Autostock/Nigel Kinrade, 29, Autostock/Russell LaBounty, 1, Cal Sports
Media, cover (bottom), NKP/John Harrelson, cover (top); Corbis: GT Images/George
Tiedemann, 20; Dreamstime: Walter Arce, 27 (all); Getty Images: Archive Photos/Bob
Harmeyer, 19, ISC Archives, 12–13, 16–17; Glow Images: Heritage Images/National
Motor Museum, 6, 7; Newscom: Everett Collection, 15, Mirrorpix, 8 (top), UPI Photo
Service/Michael Bush, 4–5; Shutterstock: Action Sports Photography, 22–23, 25;
Wikipedia: Smudge 9000, 8 (bottom), Stuart Seeger, 11, wileynorwichphoto, 10

Design Elements
Shutterstock

The publisher does not endorse products whose logos may appear on objects in
images in this book.

Printed in the United States of America in Stevens Point, Wisconsin
092014   008479WZS15

Table of Contents

FASTER THAN LIGHTNING

The light flashes green, signaling the start of the race. Race cars launch like rockets down the track. Lap after lap, the top drivers push their machines to the limit at amazing speeds. These racers use risky tactics, play mind games, and even break the rules. They want to win—or at least see their rivals lose.

Each racing series features different types of cars, rules, and point systems. In most series drivers earn points in every race for winning, finishing in the top 10, the number of laps led, and other factors. The driver with the most points at the end of the season is usually the champion. In 2014 the National Association for Stock Car Auto Racing (NASCAR) changed to a playoff format that uses points as well as a final showdown to crown the champion. Even though each series is different, they all feature fierce rivalries.

Dale Earnhardt was one of the most famous stock car drivers in history.

RACING SERIES

MAJOR RACE SERIES	CAR TYPE AND TEAM BUDGET	TYPICAL RACE COURSE	SPEED
Formula 1 (F1) • founded 1946	• **open-wheel** • custom-built • top team annual budget: about $470 million	• **road courses**; temporary street circuits • most famous: Monaco Grand Prix on the streets of Monte Carlo, Monaco; 78 laps or 161.887 miles (260.53 km)	highest official top speed: 231.523 miles (372.6 km) per hour set in 2005 by Juan Pablo Montoya
IndyCar • traces its start to United States Auto Club (USAC) founded 1956	• open-wheel • top team annual budget: about $15 million	• ovals, such as **superspeedways**; road courses; temporary street circuits • most famous: Indianapolis 500 at the Indianapolis Motor Speedway in Indiana; 200 laps or 500 miles (805 km)	highest official top speed: 241.428 miles (388.54 km) per hour set in 2000 by Gil de Ferran
National Association for Stock Car Auto Racing (NASCAR) Sprint Cup • founded 1947	• **closed-wheel** • top team annual budget: about $40 to $80 million	• ovals; superspeedways; road courses • most famous: Daytona 500 at the Daytona International Speedway, Florida; 200 laps or 500 miles (805 km)	highest official top speed: 212.809 miles (342.48 km) per hour set in 1997 by Bill Elliott

open-wheel—describes a race car with the wheels outside of the main body of the car

road course—a race that has both left and right turns and is usually held on paved tracks

superspeedway—a racetrack that is at least 2 miles (3.2 km) long

closed-wheel—describes a race car that has fenders over the wheels

A. J. FOYT VS. MARIO ANDRETTI

One of the longest racing rivalries began in the 1960s. It was between A. J. Foyt and Mario Andretti. By the end of the 1967 racing season, the two open-wheel drivers combined had won 11 of the last 12 races. Andretti won seven, and Foyt won four.

The season's last race was at Riverside International Raceway in California. Both men drove hard from the start. Then Foyt crashed his car on lap 63. But he wasn't out of the race. He took over teammate Roger McCluskey's car.

Mario Andretti

Andretti held the lead for 38 laps. But he ran low on gas and finished third. Dan Gurney passed Andretti and won. Foyt finished 17th but still earned enough points to win the season championship.

Andretti didn't win as many championships as the older Foyt. But he won more **pole positions** and led more laps. They were equally skilled rivals. In 1999 the Associated Press couldn't decide between Foyt and Andretti for "Driver of the Century." The two drivers tied.

pole position—the inside spot in the front row of cars at the beginning of a race

Foyt poses with his crew in his Lotus-Ford at the Indianapolis 500 in 1965.

DRIVER SPECS

A. J. FOYT raced from 1953 to 1994. He won the Indianapolis 500, Daytona 500, 24 Hours of Daytona, and 24 Hours of Le Mans.
- F1 race victories: 0
- F1 International Championships: 0
- holds record for most IndyCar victories: 67
- holds record for most IndyCar championships: 7
- holds record for most Indy 500 victories: 4

MARIO ANDRETTI raced from 1964 to 1994, plus one more race at Le Mans in 2000. He won the Indianapolis 500, Daytona 500, and Sebring 12-Hour Race.
- F1 race victories: 12
- F1 International Championships: 1
- IndyCar career victories: 52
- IndyCar championships: 4

NIKI LAUDA ^{VS.}
JAMES HUNT

RACING SERIES: F1

PEAK BATTLE SEASON: 1976

Niki Lauda (right) zips past his opponents in his F1 race car at the 1975 British Grand Prix.

James Hunt drives a McLaren-Ford M26 car at Brands Hatch in England during a 1978 race.

In the 1970s fans flocked to see the F1 battles between Austrian Niki Lauda and Englishman James Hunt. Niki Lauda won the international championship in 1975. James Hunt pushed hard for it in 1976. Early in the season, Hunt fell 35 points behind Lauda. Then Lauda crashed at the German Grand Prix, and his car caught fire. Hunt won the race.

Lauda missed the next three races while he healed from lung damage and burns. Hunt kept adding points. When Lauda climbed back into the driver's seat six weeks after the crash, Lauda still led Hunt by 14 points. Then Hunt won the next two races.

At the season's last race, Lauda led Hunt by just three points. That day rain soaked the track at the Japanese Grand Prix. Lauda and three other drivers withdrew from the race for safety reasons. Hunt kept racing and took third place. It was enough to win the world championship by one point! The racers' rivalry inspired the 2013 movie *Rush*.

DRIVER SPECS

JAMES HUNT raced in F1 from 1973 to 1979. He died of a heart attack in 1993 at age 45.
- pole positions: 14
- race wins: 10
- International Championships: 1

NIKI LAUDA raced in F1 from 1971 to 1985.
- pole positions: 24
- race wins: 25
- International Championships: 3

/// AYRTON SENNA VS. ALAIN PROST

RACING SERIES: F1 /// PEAK BATTLE SEASONS: 1988-90

F1 fans still take sides in the 1980s high-speed rivalry between Ayrton Senna and Alain Prost. Both men raced for the McLaren team. In 1988 Prost had scored more points, but the rules then counted points from only the best 11 results. Senna took the title instead.

Ayrton Senna

The **feud** exploded in 1989. Prost led Senna by 16 points with two races left in the season. If Senna won both remaining races, he would take the championship. In the next race, the Japanese Grand Prix, Prost crashed into Senna—or perhaps Senna turned into Prost's path. Either way, Senna was out. Prost won the title.

The two clashed again in Japan the next year. Senna led Prost by 9 points for the title and started at the pole position. Prost held the lead in the first turn. Senna tried to pass. Prost blocked him at the last second, and the pair wrecked. Damage to Prost's car forced him out. Senna won the championship.

feud—a long-running quarrel between two people or groups

Prost in his Ferrari F1-90 at the Formula 1 US Grand Prix in 1990.

DRIVER SPECS

ALAIN PROST raced in F1 from 1980 to 1991 and in the 1993 season.
- pole positions: 33
- race wins: 51
- championships: 4

AYRTON SENNA raced in F1 from 1984 to 1994, when he was killed in a crash while leading the San Marino Grand Prix in Italy.
- pole positions: 65
- race wins: 41
- championships: 3

DAVID "THE SILVER FOX" PEARSON
VS. RICHARD "THE KING" PETTY

RACING SERIES: NASCAR /// PEAK BATTLE SEASON: 1976

During the 1960s and 1970s, David Pearson and Richard Petty finished either first or second in 63 races. They often led the pack. The Daytona 500 in 1976 was no exception.

That day the two drivers exchanged the lead several times. Petty was barely ahead in the last lap. Pearson tried to **slingshot** around him. Petty blocked, and the two crashed about 20 yards (18 meters) from the finish line.

Petty and Pearson spun into the **infield**. Petty's engine died. Pearson kept his car running. He pulled onto the track, crossing the finish line at about 20 miles (32 kilometers) per hour. It's the slowest win ever for a NASCAR race.

Pearson drives toward the finish line after colliding with Petty (upper right) during the 1976 Winston Cup Daytona 500.

DRIVER SPECS

RICHARD PETTY raced in NASCAR from 1958 to 1992.
- tied with Dale Earnhardt for most NASCAR Cup championships: 7
- holds the record for most NASCAR Cup wins: 200
- holds the record for most NASCAR Cup pole positions: 123
- holds the record for most NASCAR Cup wins in a season: 27
- holds the record for most Daytona 500 wins: 7

DAVID PEARSON raced in NASCAR from 1960 to 1986.
- NASCAR Cup championships: 3
- second to Richard Petty for most NASCAR Cup wins: 105
- second to Richard Petty for most NASCAR Cup pole positions: 113
- Daytona 500 wins: 1

RICHARD PETTY VS. BOBBY ALLISON

Richard Petty had plenty of rivals during his long career. He and Bobby Allison feuded in the late 1960s and early 1970s. At North Carolina's North Wilkesboro Speedway in 1972, they bumped several times. Petty held the lead in the last laps when the two hit a wall, but they kept going. Allison then took the lead. Petty shot back in front, and they crashed into the wall again. Smoke filled Allison's car, and both bumpers fell off Petty's car. Somehow they kept going! They crashed one more time before Petty won the race.

slingshot—a move in which a trailing car uses the leading car's airflow to save energy for extra passing power

infield—the grassy area inside an oval racetrack

///CALE YARBOROUGH
vs. THE ALLISONS

RACING SERIES: NASCAR /// PEAK BATTLE SEASON: 1979

The entire Daytona 500 was broadcast on live TV for the first time in 1979. About 10 million viewers watched the action from home.

Donnie Allison led 93 of the 200 laps. With half of a lap left, Cale Yarborough tried to pass Allison on the inside. The two cars bumped hard. Yarborough dropped into the infield. He swerved onto the track, lost control, and bashed into Allison again. Both cars were wrecked, allowing Richard Petty to take the win.

Tempers flared after the race. Allison and Yarborough started fighting. Donnie's brother Bobby threw punches too. The TV cameras caught it all. Viewers at home were drawn to the rivalry. They continued to tune into the races, which helped spark NASCAR's popularity.

Bobby Allison (upper left) delivers blows to Yarborough after a collision in the final lap of the

DRIVER SPECS

CALE YARBOROUGH raced in the NASCAR Cup Series from 1957 to 1988. He also raced in four Indianapolis 500 races.
- NASCAR Cup championships: 3
- NASCAR Cup wins: 83
- Daytona 500 victories: 4

DONNIE ALLISON raced in the NASCAR Cup Series from 1966 to 1988. He also raced in two Indianapolis 500 races.
- NASCAR Cup championships: 0
- NASCAR Cup wins: 10
- Daytona 500 victories: 0

/// DARRELL WALTRIP VS. BOBBY ALLISON

RACING SERIES: **NASCAR** /// PEAK BATTLE SEASONS: **LATE 1970s**

Darrell Waltrip and Bobby Allison were friends in the early 1970s. But the 1977 Rebel 500 race at Darlington Raceway in South Carolina changed everything.

Near the end of the race, David Pearson and Richard Petty crashed. The **debris** from their cars flattened Allison's tire. It also meant a restart.

Waltrip slipped past Allison and beat him to the restart line by just 12 inches (30 centimeters) and won the race. Allison was furious. The two men have rarely spoken to each other since.

debris—the scattered pieces of something that has been broken or destroyed

Waltrip (88) races against Allison at the Talladega Superspeedway in 1979.

DRIVER SPECS

DARRELL WALTRIP raced in NASCAR from 1972 to 2000. He then became a TV racing commentator. His first TV job was the 2001 Daytona 500. Waltrip's younger brother Michael won that race.
- NASCAR Cup championships: 3
- NASCAR Cup wins: 84
- NASCAR Cup pole positions: 59
- Daytona 500 victories: 1

BOBBY ALLISON raced in the NASCAR Cup Series from 1961 to 1988. He also raced in two Indianapolis 500 races. He finished second in the NASCAR Cup championship five times.
- NASCAR Cup championships: 1
- NASCAR Cup wins: 84—tied with Darrell Waltrip
- NASCAR Cup pole positions: 58
- Daytona 500 victories: 3

DALE EARNHARDT vs.
DARRELL WALTRIP (1986)
vs. JEFF GORDON (1995)

RACING SERIES: NASCAR /// PEAK BATTLE SEASONS: 1980s–1990s

Dale Earnhardt's reckless style was not wreck-less! He earned the name "The Intimidator" for the way he blocked, **drafted**, and bumped his way to Victory Lane.

Earnhardt had many rivals in his career, including Darrell Waltrip. In 1986 at Richmond International Speedway, Earnhardt and Waltrip bumped into each other with about 15 laps to go. Waltrip shot past him. Just when it looked like Waltrip could win, Earnhardt spun Waltrip into the wall, causing a four-vehicle wreck. Earnhardt's car was damaged, but he took third place. Racing officials fined Earnhardt $5,000 for reckless driving. The fine was later reduced to $3,000.

The two drivers battled on the track again and again. But off the track, they later became friends.

draft—to follow closely behind another race car

THE FAMOUS "PASS IN THE GRASS"

In 1987 Dale Earnhardt took an early lead at The Winston, a 90-lap invitational race. During the final 10 laps, Bill Elliott caught Earnhardt, who blocked every pass attempt. Then they smashed bumpers. The move pushed Earnhardt off the track and into the infield. Earnhardt pulled back onto the course and kept his lead to the finish line. Even though Earnhardt didn't actually pass Elliott in the infield, people started calling the incident "the pass in the grass." Elliott was furious with Earnhardt after the race. But Earnhardt didn't apologize—he said it was all part of racing.

Earnhardt (2) and Waltrip drive neck and neck at the 1980 Atlanta 500.

invitational—an event that selects the best drivers to compete

Earnhardt (left) and Gordon eye each other before the Pennsylvania 500 at Pocono International Speedway in 1997.

By 1995 Earnhardt was the **veteran** racer. He had won a record seven NASCAR Cup titles. Early in the season, he was doing well in points. Then he fell behind 23-year-old driver Jeff Gordon.

At the Indianapolis Brickyard 400, Gordon won the pole and took an early lead. Earnhardt let the other drivers swap the lead until lap 133. Then Earnhardt charged ahead and held off the other cars to win by just .37 of a second. Gordon finished sixth.

That season Earnhardt won two more races. So did Gordon. Gordon beat Earnhardt for the Cup championship by just 34 points. The rivalry continued until Earnhardt's death in 2001. In 2014 Gordon said he always looked up to Earnhardt and considered him a friend.

DRIVER SPECS

DALE EARNHARDT raced from 1975 to 2001, when he was killed in a crash on the last lap of the Daytona 500.
- NASCAR Cup championships: 7 (tied with Richard Petty for the record)
- NASCAR Cup wins: 76
- NASCAR Cup pole positions: 22
- Daytona 500 victories: 1

JEFF GORDON started racing in the NASCAR Cup Series at age 20 in 1992.
- NASCAR Cup championships: 4
- NASCAR Cup wins: 92
- NASCAR Cup pole positions: 76
- Daytona 500 victories: 3

veteran—someone who has a lot of experience in a particular job or activity

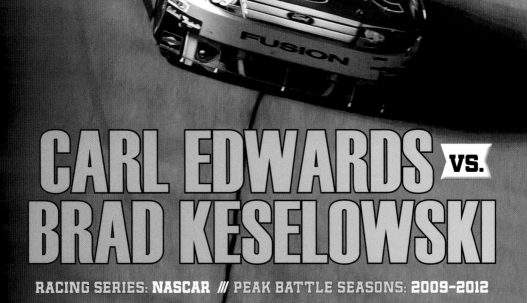

CARL EDWARDS VS. BRAD KESELOWSKI

RACING SERIES: NASCAR /// PEAK BATTLE SEASONS: 2009-2012

Fans enjoy Carl Edwards' exciting victory back flips from the window ledge of his car. But in 2009 at Talladega, his car did the flipping.

Edwards was leading when Brad Keselowski bumped him near the finish line. Edwards' car sailed into the safety fence, bounced to the infield, and burst into flames. Debris from the car and fence caused minor injuries to seven fans nearby. Edwards safely escaped the car and ran the last few yards to cross the finish line. It didn't count, but fans loved it!

Keselowski and Edwards have clashed since they first met racing trucks in the early 2000s.

CARL EDWARDS started racing in the NASCAR Cup Series in 2004 at age 24. He has twice placed second in Cup championship points, in 2008 and 2011.

- NASCAR Cup championships: 0
- NASCAR Cup wins: 23
- NASCAR pole positions: 13

BRAD KESELOWSKI started racing in the NASCAR Cup Series in 2008 at age 24.

- NASCAR Cup championships: 1
- NASCAR Cup wins: 15
- NASCAR Cup pole positions: 8

Edwards (far left) and Keselowski bring their cars down the frontstretch at the 2010 Emory Healthcare 500 at Atlanta Motor Speedway.

After the wreck at Talladega, the rivalry flared up again in 2012 at the Atlanta Motor Speedway. Early in the race Edwards and Keselowski banged into each other. Edwards needed repairs. He finally pulled onto the track at lap 153. Keselowski was near the lead. During the last three laps, Edwards nudged him. Keselowski's car ended up on its front wheels and then flipped into the fence. Fortunately, no one was hurt.

Keselowski said later that season that the rivalry was over. But fans aren't so sure.

JEFF GORDON VS.
JIMMIE JOHNSON

RACING SERIES: NASCAR /// PEAK BATTLE SEASONS: 2002-CURRENT

Jeff Gordon signed Jimmie Johnson to his racing team in 2002. Both talented drivers had joined the NASCAR Cup Series in their 20s. They soon became friends. But their competitive personalities later sparked trouble.

At Texas Motor Speedway in April 2010, the two drivers made contact on the track, and their rivalry exploded. Their conflict kept both of them from winning. Then at Talladega the following week, Johnson blocked Gordon and pushed him to the inside **apron**. The move caused a huge pile-up. Since then these two former friends haven't shown any signs of backing off.

apron—the low, inside paved area of a racetrack

Gordon (24), Johnson (48), and Keselowski (12) race three wide at Talladega Superspeedway in 2010.

DRIVER SPECS

JEFF GORDON started racing in the NASCAR Cup Series at age 20 in 1992.
- NASCAR Cup championships: 4
- NASCAR Cup wins: 92
- NASCAR Cup pole positions: 76
- Daytona 500 victories: 3

JIMMIE JOHNSON started racing in the NASCAR Cup Series in 2001 at age 25. He holds the record for winning the most Cup championships in a row, from 2006 through 2010.
- NASCAR Cup championships: 6
- NASCAR Cup wins: 69
- NASCAR Cup pole positions: 33
- Daytona 500 victories: 2

/// DANICA PATRICK vs. THE GUYS

Danica Patrick (7) surges by her opponents at the Auto Club Speedway in California in 2010.

Danica Patrick moved from open-wheel racing to stock car racing in 2010. She moved up to NASCAR's Cup Series full-time in 2013. She was the first woman to earn a pole at that level when she claimed it at the 2013 Daytona 500.

The media and others have questioned if Patrick's small size is an unfair advantage compared to the men drivers. Less weight means more speed in racing. She weighs about 100 pounds (45 kilograms). NASCAR assumes men weigh more than 140 pounds (64 kg). But nobody questioned if Mark Martin had an advantage when he won 40 races. He weighed about 125 pounds (57 kg).

Before the 2014 season, Richard Petty upset Patrick's fans by suggesting that the only way she would win a NASCAR race was if everyone else stayed home. Can Patrick prove she has the driving skills to win? Many racers and fans are cheering for her!

DRIVER SPECS

DANICA PATRICK started racing in the IndyCar Series in 2005. She raced part-time in the NASCAR Nationwide stock car series in 2010. She moved to NASCAR's Cup Series part-time in 2012 and raced her first full season there in 2013.

- IndyCar wins: 1
- first woman to win an IndyCar race
- IndyCar Series Rookie of the Year in 2005
- IndyCar pole positions: 4
- NASCAR Cup pole positions: 1

DALE EARNHARDT JR.
VS. KASEY KAHNE

RACING SERIES: NASCAR /// **PEAK BATTLE SEASONS: 2003-CURRENT**

Who is more popular—Dale Earnhardt Jr. or Kasey Kahne? Fans have voted for Earnhardt Jr. as the Most Popular Driver 11 years in a row since 2003. That's more than any other driver in NASCAR Cup history. But Kahne's experience and racing style have pushed him to the top ranks in the sport.

Who's the better driver? Earnhardt and Kahne both have strong track records. They drive for the same Hendrick Motorsports team as Jeff Gordon and Jimmie Johnson. Both drivers would love to leave those two champions in the dust. They have the talent. Do they have the luck?

DRIVER SPECS

DALE EARNHARDT JR. began racing full-time in the NASCAR Cup Series in 2000.
- NASCAR Cup championships: 0
- NASCAR Cup wins: 22
- NASCAR Cup pole positions: 13
- NASCAR's Most Popular Driver award: 2003–2013
- Daytona 500 wins: 1

KASEY KAHNE started racing in open-wheel cars when he was 17. In 2004 he took second place five times in his first full NASCAR Cup season.
- NASCAR Cup championships: 0
- NASCAR Cup wins: 17
- NASCAR Cup pole positions: 26
- NASCAR Rookie of the Year in 2004

Kasey Kahne (left) and Dale Earnhardt Jr. talk during practice at the 2012 NASCAR Sprint Cup Series race at Talladega.

FANTASTIC FEUDS

Rivalries shift into high gear during each racing season. They're often settled at the finish line by split seconds and a dash of luck. But some rivalries keep simmering and never really seem to be settled. It's these surprises that keep racing fans coming back for more thrilling racing action.

Glossary

apron (AY-pruhn)—the low, inside paved area of a racetrack

closed-wheel (KLOHZD-weel)—describes a race car that has fenders over the wheels

debris (duh-BREE)—the scattered pieces of something that has been broken or destroyed

draft (DRAFT)—to follow closely behind another race car

feud (FYOOD)—a long-running quarrel between two people or groups of people

infield (IN-feeld)—the grassy area inside an oval racetrack

invitational (in-vi-TAY-shuhn-uhl)—an event that selects the best drivers to compete

open-wheel (OH-puhn-WEEL)—describes a race car with the wheels outside of the main body of the car

pole position (POHL puh-ZISH-uhn)—the inside spot in the front row of cars at the beginning of a race

road course (ROHD KORSS)—a race that has both left and right turns and is usually held on paved tracks

slingshot (SLING-shot)—a move in which a trailing car uses the leading car's airflow to save energy for extra passing power

superspeedway (soo-pur-SPEED-way)—a racetrack that is at least 2 miles (3.2 km) long

veteran (VET-ur-uhn)—someone who has a lot of experience in a particular job or activity

Read More

Howard, Melanie A. *Stock Cars*. Full Throttle. North Mankato, Minn.: Capstone Press, 2011.

Kopp, Megan. *NASCAR*. The Greatest Players. New York: AV2 by Weigl, 2014.

Murray, Robb. *A Daredevil's Guide to Car Racing*. Daredevils' Guides. North Mankato, Minn.: Capstone Press, 2013.

Internet Sites

FactHound offers a safe, fun way to find Internet sites related to this book. All of the sites on FactHound have been researched by our staff.

Here's all you do:

Visit *www.facthound.com*

Type in this code: 9781491420256

Check out projects, games and lots more at
www.capstonekids.com

Index

CYRENIUS H. BOOTH LIBRARY

3 4014 13301 2204

Cyrenius H. Booth Library
25 Main Street
Newtown, CT 06470